OLYMPIC SPORTS

OLYMPIC SOCCER

BY CHRÖS McDOUGALL

SportsZone
An Imprint of Abdo Publishing
abdobooks.com

abdobooks.com

Published by Abdo Publishing, a division of ABDO, PO Box 398166, Minneapolis, Minnesota 55439.

Printed in the United States of America, North Mankato, Minnesota.
102024
012025

THIS BOOK CONTAINS RECYCLED MATERIALS

Cover Photo: Brad Smith/ISI/Getty Images Sport/Getty Images
Interior Photos: Doug Pensinger/Allsport/Getty Images Sport/Getty Images, 5; David Madison/Getty Images Sport/Getty Images, 6; David Cannon/David Cannon Collection/Getty Images, 8, 29; IOP/AFP/Getty Images, 9; Michel Lipchitz/AP Images, 11; David Cannon/Allsport/David Cannon Collection/Getty Images, 12; Apic/Bridgeman/Hulton Archive/Getty Images, 15; S&G/PA Images Archive/Getty Images, 16; ullstein bild Dtl./Getty Images, 18; Peter Robinson/EMPICS/PA Images/Getty Images, 19; Robert Cianflone/Getty Images Sport/Getty Images, 22, 45; Central Press/Hulton Archive/Getty Images, 25; AFP/Getty Images, 26; Robert Cianflone/Allsport/Getty Images Sport/Getty Images, 30; Stuart Franklin/FIFA/Getty Images, 32; Carl Recine/Getty Images Sport/Getty Images, 35; Franck Seguin/Corbis Sport/VCG/Getty Images, 37; Pedro Ugarte/AFP/Getty Images, 38; Michael Regan/Getty Images Sport/Getty Images, 41; Naomi Baker/Getty Images Sport/Getty Images, 43

Editor: Haley Williams
Series Designer: Karli Kruse

Library of Congress Control Number: 2024938405

Publisher's Cataloging-in-Publication Data

Names: McDougall, Chrös, author.
Title: Olympic soccer / by Chrös McDougall
Description: Minneapolis, Minnesota: ABDO Publishing, 2025 | Series: Olympic sports | Includes online resources and index.
Identifiers: ISBN 9781098295509 (lib. bdg.) | ISBN 9798384916505 (ebook)
Subjects: LCSH: Olympic games--Juvenile literature. | European football--Juvenile literature. | Soccer—Juvenile literature. | Olympians (Olympic athletes)--Juvenile literature. | Olympics--History--Juvenile literature. | Sports--Juvenile literature.
Classification: DDC 796.334--dc23

TABLE OF CONTENTS

CHAPTER 1

A GOLDEN DEBUT

Tiffeny Milbrett has always been small but relentless. Growing up in Oregon, Milbrett became a star point guard in basketball. She qualified for the high school state track-and-field championships as a sprinter and long jumper. But where she really stood out was on the soccer field.

Milbrett exploded past defenders with ease. All she wanted to do was score goals. And as a senior in 1989, she scored 54 of them. That set a state record. And she did it in just 14 games. It was little surprise when she won her third straight Oregon high school player of the year award. But Milbrett was already dreaming bigger. That season, her coach asked about her goals as a soccer player. Milbrett responded that she wanted to play in the Olympic Games. But there was one problem: women's soccer was not an Olympic sport.

Tiffeny Milbrett, *in white*, joined the US women's national team in 1991.

THE ROAD TO ATLANTA

By the 1990s, soccer had enjoyed a long Olympic history. However, that history didn't include women. The wheels were in motion to change that, though. Women's soccer had grown in popularity throughout the 1970s and 1980s. In 1991, the first Women's World Cup was held in China. And two years after that, Olympic officials voted to make women's soccer a medal event. The sport would make its debut at the 1996 Games in Atlanta.

Most of the US players who competed at the first Women's World Cup in 1991 were also members of the first Olympic team five years later.

This timing proved to be ideal for Milbrett and the home team. Women's soccer had particularly taken off in the United States during the early 1990s. The hard-charging US team took home the championship at the first Women's World Cup. Then, with Milbrett as a key member, the team finished third in the tournament in 1995. One year later, Milbrett was one of 16 women named to the first US Olympic women's soccer team. Her teenage dream had come true.

The Americans came into the 1996 Games as a favorite to win. By then, the core group of players had been together for years. Milbrett and striker Mia Hamm made up an elite forward line. If one of them was not scoring, they were assisting the other. But winning the first Olympic gold medal wasn't going to be easy. Norway had won the previous year's Women's World Cup. And all the teams at the Olympics had to navigate a tight schedule. During the group stage, each team had to play three games in five days.

THE GAMES BEGIN

The first sign that Olympic women's soccer could be a success came in the United States' opening game. During the Olympics, soccer games often take place away from the host city. The 1996 women's opener was set for July 21 in Orlando, Florida. Despite temperatures nearing 100 degrees Fahrenheit (38°C),

Fans from around the world cheered on the eight teams participating in the 1996 Olympic women's soccer tournament.

more than 25,000 fans came out to see the United States play Denmark. Milbrett scored the third goal in a 3–0 victory.

A similar crowd showed up to the next US game, also in Orlando. This time the Americans held off Sweden, 2–1. However, Hamm left the game with an ankle injury. She missed the next game, too. It ended as a 0–0 draw with China. Playing three games in five days left the players exhausted. But off the field, the tournament was a big hit. The Americans' third game drew 43,525 fans to the stadium in Miami, Florida.

Sanford Stadium in Athens, Georgia, is the home of the University of Georgia football team. But on July 28, a crowd of 64,196 people filed in for the Olympic women's semifinal soccer games. Most were there to cheer on Team USA. And the Americans were about to face their biggest test yet. Norway had always played the United States tough. The US team beat Norway in the 1991 Women's World Cup final. But Norway got revenge in the 1995 semifinals. Now the Norwegians were eager to knock off the United States again.

The game got off to a promising start for the Norwegians. Defender Linda Medalen scored on a long shot to put Norway

Norway's Ann Kristin Aarønes, *right*, was one of the top scorers at the 1996 Olympics with four goals.

WAITING TO WATCH

Historic crowds followed the US women's soccer team at the 1996 Olympics. However, watching the Games on TV was harder back then. On a busy night, NBC showed only 20 minutes of the final. But 25 years later, the network made the full game available to stream. Members of the US team also took part in a documentary about the Atlanta Games.

up 1–0 in the 18th minute. Meanwhile, the US team appeared stuck. Hamm had returned to the lineup. An energetic crowd cheered the Americans on. But the team struggled to break through. With 20 minutes to play, the United States still had not scored.

Finally, the home team got a break. Around the 76th minute, the Americans played a ball into Norway's penalty area. It grazed a Norwegian player's hand. The referee awarded the United States a penalty kick. Team USA's Michelle Akers then drilled the shot to tie the game 1–1. Things only unraveled from there for Norway.

Ten minutes later, a Norwegian player was ejected after committing a rough foul on Hamm. That left Norway with only 10 players. In extra time, the Americans took advantage. Ten minutes in, US midfielder Julie Foudy got the ball in open space. The speedy Shannon MacMillan then cut toward the goal. Foudy slipped a pass right into MacMillan's path. MacMillan sent the ball into the goal, ending the game. The United States moved on to the final with a 2–1 victory.

Shannon MacMillan, *right*, of the United States watches her game-winning shot beat Norwegian goalkeeper Bente Nordby in the 1996 Olympic semifinals.

GOING FOR THE GOLD

The 1996 Games were a breakthrough event for American women in many sports. US teams had already won gold medals in gymnastics and softball. The women's basketball team was on the way to gold as well. And on August 1, another huge crowd returned to Sanford Stadium to see if the women's soccer team could join the party.

The United States celebrates after defeating China to win its first Olympic gold medal in women's soccer.

The final test was a big one, though. Behind star forward Sun Wen, China had played well all tournament. The Americans knew they would have to come out hard. And that is what they did. In the 18th minute, the US players charged toward China's goal. Hamm took a shot that bounced off the post. The rebound flew right to a wide-open MacMillan for an easy goal.

The goal seemed to wake China up. The team clamped down on the Americans. Then, in the 32nd minute, Sun got behind the US defenders and chipped in the game-tying goal.

China continued to control the game into the second half. But with the crowd behind them, the Americans pushed back. In the 68th minute, they found an opening. Hamm started the attack from the right wing. Under pressure, she passed forward. Joy Fawcett outran a defender to reach the ball. Then Fawcett sent it across the goal area and into the path of a charging and wide open Milbrett.

Milbrett had scored countless goals in her career. And with a women's soccer record crowd of 76,481 fans looking on, she wasn't going to miss that one. With a calm right-footed kick, she sent the ball into the net. Twenty minutes later, Milbrett's goal held up in a 2–1 win. Seven years after her impossible dream, Milbrett had become an Olympian. And her goal had secured the United States the first Olympic gold medal in women's soccer.

CHAPTER 2

OLYMPIC SOCCER THROUGH THE YEARS

The first organized soccer games took place among students in England during the mid-1800s. By the end of the century, the game had spread to countries around the world. Around the same time, a French educator named Pierre de Coubertin was learning about the ancient Greek Olympics. Inspired, Coubertin began a movement to create a new international sporting festival. And in 1896, his vision became a reality. The first modern Olympic Games were held that year in Athens, Greece.

The new Olympics would be held every four years. A men's soccer tournament was included in the 1900 Games in Paris, France, and the 1904 Games in St. Louis. However, those tournaments featured club teams. Because of that, soccer's governing body considers 1908 to be the first official Olympic soccer tournament.

Early Olympics were not as sophisticated as they are today. That showed in 1908. Two of the eight teams couldn't afford the trip to London, England, and withdrew. In one game,

Pierre de Coubertin founded the International Olympic Committee and served as its president from 1896 to 1925.

Denmark beat France 17–1. Forward Sophus Nielsen scored an amazing 10 goals in that game.

In the end, it came down to Denmark and Great Britain for the gold medal. In front of 8,000 fans, Great Britain's captain Vivian Woodward led his team to a 2–0 victory. Then, four years later at the 1912 Games, he did it again. This time Woodward and Great Britain beat Denmark 4–2 in Stockholm, Sweden.

Soccer was rapidly growing across the world during the early 1900s. By 1920, the Olympic tournament had 14 teams.

At the 1908 Olympics, Great Britain outscored its opponents 18–1 across three games to win gold.

Among them was Egypt, the first team from outside Europe to compete in Olympic soccer. Four years later, Uruguay became the first South American participant. Not only did Uruguay win, but then it won again in 1928. A crowd of 25,250 watched the 1928 final in Amsterdam, Netherlands.

A NEW ERA

Soccer had become a hit at the Olympics. But to soccer officials, this meant the sport was outgrowing the Games. They believed soccer should have its own stand-alone championship event. And so two years later, in 1930, the first World Cup was held in Uruguay. Olympic soccer would never be the same after that.

From the start, the World Cup became the premier championship for men's soccer. This created tension among Olympic officials. They pulled the sport out of the 1932 Games in Los Angeles. That remains the only Olympics since 1896 to not include soccer. Olympic officials agreed to bring soccer back for the 1936 Games in Berlin, Germany. However, the tournament would be distinctly different from the World Cup.

There had been another important reason for creating the World Cup. In those days, the Olympics were for amateur athletes. However, the best soccer players were increasingly joining professional club teams. These players were allowed

The 1936 Olympic soccer tournament was held in what is now the Berlin Olympic Stadium. The stadium is still used today for international soccer games.

to play in the World Cup. The Olympics, on the other hand, remained the sport's amateur championship.

Like many sporting events, the Olympics were canceled during World War II (1939–1945). In the years that followed, a split occurred within soccer. Countries from South America and western Europe emerged as powers at the World Cup. But at the Olympics, teams from the Eastern Bloc dominated. The Eastern Bloc was a group of countries in eastern Europe that had close ties to the Soviet Union. From 1952 to 1980, countries from this area of the world won 22 of the 25 medals awarded for soccer. That included all eight golds. A big reason why was these nations' ability to work around amateurism. In many Eastern Bloc countries, top athletes were given government jobs. This allowed those athletes to train at a high level. But since they were not technically paid for being athletes, they were still considered amateurs.

Poland, *in white*, and Spain compete in the men's soccer final at the 1992 Games in Barcelona, Spain. Spain won 3–2 to capture its first Olympic gold medal in soccer.

GOLD AROUND THE GLOBE

In the 22 men's World Cups from 1930 through 2022, eight countries have won. Meanwhile, the nine Olympic Games from 1992 to 2024 produced six different men's winners. Notably, all the World Cup winners have come from Europe or South America. No African or North American countries have even reached a World Cup final. But Cameroon, Mexico, and Nigeria have all won Olympic gold medals since 1996.

Finally, in 1984, the Olympics began allowing some professional soccer players to take part. Eventually these rules were relaxed further. Then, in 1992, the Olympics switched to a new format. Soccer players had to be age 23 or younger. Starting in 1996, each team could include three players older than 23. Those rules have been in place ever since.

The Under-23 (U23) format is unusual for Olympic sports. Club soccer teams can also prevent their players from taking part in the Olympics. Because of these rules, fans are sometimes not sure what to make of the tournament's importance.

However, many fans embrace these quirks. They enjoy seeing so many talented young players in a competitive environment. Olympic soccer is also often unpredictable. Teams that have never come close to winning a World Cup have won Olympic medals. These factors make Olympic soccer a unique event.

THE WOMEN'S GAME

Coubertin had a grand vision for the Olympic Games. He believed the event could bring the world together. Instead of fighting on battlefields, countries could compete against one another in sports. However, that vision did not include women. At least, it didn't right away.

No women took part in the first Olympics in 1896. A handful of women competed in the 1900 Games. But men still outnumbered women by more than 50 to one. Coubertin didn't believe sports were appropriate for women. And he was not alone in that thinking. Women have had to fight for more opportunities in sports for many years.

Access to girls' and women's sports began to really pick up during the 1970s. By the 1990s, a generation of young women had grown up playing sports. This led to a breakthrough at the Olympics.

In 1996, a record 3,517 women took part in the Atlanta Games. That was nearly 800 more than in the 1992 Games in Barcelona, Spain. It was the biggest jump ever. A big reason for this increase was the addition of two new Olympic women's sports: softball and soccer.

No women's sport attracted more fans than soccer. Unlike in men's soccer, there was no age limit for the women's tournament. National teams could all field their countries'

An average of 9 million Americans tuned in to watch the 2024 Olympic women's soccer final between the United States and Brazil.

best players. And in 1996, those players were hungry for opportunities. This led to an exciting, competitive tournament.

The Olympics immediately became the second major championship in women's soccer, behind only the Women's World Cup. And over the years, the Olympic tournament has only continued to grow. On the field, many of the sport's most legendary players have won Olympic medals. Growth has come off the field, too. The 2012 Olympics were back in London. An Olympic-record crowd of 80,203 people came out to watch the gold-medal match at the famous Wembley Stadium. Only 100 years earlier, women were mostly kept out of the Games. In the short history of women's soccer, the athletes have shown they very much belong.

STILL NOT EQUAL

The Olympic soccer tournament is more important for the women's side than the men's. However, women's Olympic soccer is still not treated equally. At the 2024 Games in Paris, the men's soccer tournament had 16 teams. But only 12 teams took part in the women's tournament.

CHAPTER 3

MEN'S GREATS

British railway workers introduced soccer to Uruguay in the late 1800s. Over the following years, the small South American country found success in its region. To Europeans, however, Uruguay remained an unknown. The team's arrival at the 1924 Olympic Games in Paris began a new era in soccer.

That year's tournament featured 22 teams from four continents. Many people consider it to be soccer's first truly global championship. And from their opening 7–0 win over Yugoslavia, the Uruguayans stole the show.

Led by captain José Nasazzi, the Uruguayans raced around the field. Their playing style, based on short passes, took opponents by surprise. Opposing players seemed to be standing still next to the fast-moving Uruguayans. One reporter described their advanced style as "playing chess with their feet."

Uruguay's José Nasazzi, *front right*, defends Argentina's Enrique Gainzarain during the gold-medal match at the 1928 Olympics.

Ferenc Puskás began playing for the Hungarian national soccer team in 1945.

No Uruguayan captured interest quite like José Leandro Andrade. During that time, soccer was mostly a segregated sport. Andrade, who was Black, became a sensation. When he took the field, Andrade's effortless, dynamic play seemed to captivate people. Uruguay beat Switzerland 3–0 to win gold. Four years later at the 1928 Olympics, many of those same players helped Uruguay win again. This time they outlasted neighbor and rival Argentina in the final in Amsterdam.

THE GOLDEN TEAM

Any list of the greatest soccer players ever is sure to include Ferenc Puskás. The Hungarian striker averaged almost a goal per game for his national team. And many of his goals were spectacular. The one mark against Puskás is that he and the powerful Hungarian team never won a World Cup. The Olympics were a different story, though.

The 1940 and 1944 Olympics had been canceled due to World War II. Hungary didn't take part in the 1948 Olympics in London or the 1950 World Cup. But in June of 1950, the team began an unbeaten run. That run continued into the 1952 Olympics in Helsinki, Finland. With an attack-minded approach, the Hungarians tore through the tournament.

In the semifinals, Hungary turned aside defending champion Sweden 6–0. Then Puskás scored his fourth goal of the tournament in the final against Yugoslavia. His team went on to win 2–0. The group was nicknamed the "Golden Team."

Those Games were Puskás's lone trip to the Olympics. But Hungary won a bronze medal in 1960. That was followed by two more gold medals in 1964

LEV YASHIN

Lev Yashin was nicknamed "Black Spider." In his famous all-black uniform, the Soviet goalie seemed to stop everything. Many people still consider him the best to ever play the position. Like Ferenc Puskás, Yashin never won a World Cup. But also like Puskás, he did win Olympic gold. Yashin gave up just two goals during the Soviet Union's gold-medal run at the 1956 Games in Melbourne, Australia.

and 1968, and then a silver in 1972. That is still the most successful 20-year stretch in Olympic men's soccer history.

AFRICAN ARRIVAL

For many years, African countries rarely contended for major international soccer championships. That began to change at the 1988 Olympics in Seoul, South Korea. That year, Zambia beat Guatemala 4–0 during the group stage. Four years later, in the first U23 Olympic tournament, Ghana claimed the bronze medal. It was the first soccer medal for an African country.

In 1996, Nigeria took the next step. The team, known as the Super Eagles, was rich in talent. The Nigerians were hardly favorites to win, though. Their country was experiencing political turmoil. Between games, the players had to cram into a cheap motel. But once they got on the field, the Super Eagles took over.

Fans rallied around the exciting squad. With two wins, Nigeria advanced out of the group stage for the first time. Then the team beat Mexico 2–0 in the quarterfinals. The semifinals brought a rematch with Brazil. The South Americans had edged Nigeria 1–0 in the group stage finale. Round two started much worse for the Super Eagles. Brazil scored in the first minute, then added two more goals by halftime. Trailing 3–1, Nigeria's lone tally had come on an own goal.

That score held as the second half ticked on. Then, in the 78th minute, Nigeria's Victor Ikpeba scored to bring his team within one. Then Nigeria captain Nwankwo Kanu tied the game in the 90th minute. That sent the game into extra time. Four minutes later, Kanu received a pass from midfield. He faked

Nwankwo Kanu, *right*, of Nigeria keeps the ball from Brazil's Roberto Carlos during the men's semifinals at the 1996 Games.

out a defender, then scored the game-winning goal. The Super Eagles completed their historic run a few days later with a 3–2 win over Argentina. Their victory set off a national celebration back home.

Four years later at the 2000 Olympics in Sydney, Australia, it was Cameroon's turn. The Indomitable Lions struggled to get out of the group stage. But when they did, they began rolling. In the quarterfinals, Cameroon snuck past Brazil in extra time. Then the team beat Chile 2–1 in the semis. That set up a gold-medal showdown with Spain. With nearly 105,000 fans in attendance, Cameroon went down 2–0 in the first half. But the Lions got one back on an own goal. Five minutes later, the talented 19-year-old forward Samuel Eto'o tied it.

The Indomitable Lions of Cameroon pose with their gold medals after beating Spain in the 2000 Olympic men's final. It was the first Olympic soccer medal Cameroon had ever won.

Finally, Cameroon completed the comeback with a shootout win to earn the gold medal.

ARGENTINA'S STARS

At the 2008 Olympics in Beijing, China, no team could match the star power of Argentina's squad. Legendary playmaker Juan Román Riquelme was an over-23 player. Among his teammates were Lionel Messi, Sergio Agüero, and Ángel Di Maria. Riquelme and the future superstars led Argentina past Nigeria for the country's second Olympic gold medal.

BRAZIL'S TIME

The Brazilian players walked onto the field at London's Wembley Stadium with confidence. Brazil was a proud soccer country. It had a super talented team at the 2012 Olympics. Neymar, the team's fearless 20-year-old forward, was one of the brightest young talents in the game. All Brazil needed to do was defeat underdog Mexico in the final. A win would secure the last major championship Brazil had yet to claim.

Instead, Mexico's Oribe Peralta scored 29 seconds into the game. Then he scored again in the 75th minute. Brazil got one back in stoppage time. But it was too late. Mexico won 2–1. Neymar and his teammates sat on the field, stunned.

Two years later, Brazil suffered an even bigger heartbreak. The country was hosting the 2014 World Cup. Locals dreamed of lifting the famous World Cup trophy in Rio de Janeiro, Brazil.

Neymar scored eight goals during his two Olympic appearances in 2012 and 2016.

Instead, with Neymar out injured, Brazil fell 7–1 to Germany in the semifinals. It matched the worst defeat ever for Brazil.

In 2016, the Olympics came to Rio de Janeiro. By then, Neymar was 24 years old. That put him above the U23 age limit. But Neymar remembered watching the Olympics as a child. He dreamed of leading his country to its first gold medal on home soil. So he joined the Olympic team as one of its three over-23 players and as its captain.

The quest for gold began poorly. Brazil opened with 0–0 draws against South Africa and Iraq. A 4–0 win over Denmark got things rolling. Then Brazil shut out Colombia 2–0 and Honduras 6–0 to reach the final. It was a rematch with Germany.

A crowd of 78,000 showed up at the famous Maracanã Stadium in Rio. Fans roared in the 28th minute when Neymar curled a free kick into the goal. It was his fourth goal of the tournament. But Germany tied the game a half hour later. The score remained deadlocked at 1–1 through extra time. That meant it would be decided by a shootout.

After eight shots, the shootout remained tied 4–4. Brazil's goalie then stopped Germany's fifth attempt with a diving save. That sent Neymar to the spot with a chance to win. Fans across Brazil held their breath. Neymar kissed the ball and placed it on the grass. On a long run-up, he made a dramatic stutter step. Then, he struck a right-footed shot. It sailed safely into the upper corner of the net. Once again, Neymar ended the gold-medal game on his knees. This time, however, he cried tears of joy. Brazil, at long last, was the Olympic champion.

INSTANT CLASSIC

French athletes had given the country a lot to cheer for at the 2024 Olympics in Paris. On Friday August 9, fans packed into the Parc des Princes ready for more. They were treated to an instant classic.

Enzo Millot put the home team up early. But Spain, the defending silver medalists, came roaring back. Fermín López scored twice in eight minutes. Then Álex Baena's free kick goal put Spain up 3–1. And it was still only the 28th minute.

That score remained until the 79th minute, when chaos took over again. With a passionate crowd behind them, France's Maghnes Akliouche and Jean-Philippe Mateta each scored to send the game to extra time. But the game ended in heartbreak for the home fans.

DOUBLING UP

Malcom scored in extra time to send Brazil past Spain in the Tokyo, Japan, Olympics in 2021. That made Brazil the fifth men's team to win back-to-back gold medals in soccer. It joined Great Britain (1908, 1912), Uruguay (1924, 1928), Hungary (1964, 1968), and Argentina (2004, 2008).

France's Castello Lukeba, *left*, and Spain's Fermín López fight for the ball during the men's gold-medal match at the 2024 Games.

Sergio Camello's two extra time goals gave Spain a 5–3 win. It was the first gold medal for a European team since Spain's win at the 1992 Games.

The result wasn't what the French players had hoped for. But the teams had put on a remarkable show in the highest-scoring Olympic men's final ever. After the game, fans cheered loudly as the home team took a lap around the field.

CHAPTER 4

WOMEN'S GREATS

The 1996 Olympics had shown women's soccer could draw big crowds. The 1999 Women's World Cup took that to another level. Playing on home soil, the United States packed stadiums around the country. More than 90,000 people came out to watch the final. In a thrilling shootout, the Americans clinched their second championship.

Much of the same team was back for the Olympics the following year in Sydney. And an old rival was waiting. The Americans met Norway in the gold-medal match. They got off to a fast start. Tiffeny Milbrett, the star of the 1996 Olympics, put Team USA up five minutes into the game. But Norway tied it just before halftime. Then, in the 78th minute, Ragnhild Gulbrandsen put the Norwegians up 2–1.

The thrilling, back-and-forth game came down to the closing seconds. On what might have been the final attack, Mia Hamm sent a cross in front of Norway's goal.

Mia Hamm finished her US women's national team career with 158 goals and 144 assists.

Milbrett, though just 5-foot-2, leaped into the air to head in the tying goal.

The storybook comeback was not to be for the US team, though. Twelve minutes into extra time, Norway sent a long pass toward the US goal. A US defender tried to head it away. Instead, the ball bounced to Norway's Dagny Mellgren. Her well-placed shot skidded past the diving US goalie to secure Norway's first gold medal in Olympic soccer.

A GOLDEN TRIFECTA

For years, Brandi Chastain, Mia Hamm, Joy Fawcett, Julie Foudy, and Kristine Lilly made up the backbone of the US women's

Norway's Dagny Mellgren, *left*, beats US goalie Siri Mullinix during the women's gold-medal match at the 2000 Olympics.

national team. They all joined the squad as teenagers in the late 1980s. The "Fab Five," as they were often called, won a pair of Women's World Cups and the 1996 Olympic gold medal together. By the 2004 Olympics in Athens, Greece, the Fab Five were all in their 30s. Hamm, Fawcett, and Foudy planned to retire after the Games. That meant it would be the last tournament with all five of them. They were determined to go out on top.

For the third Olympics in a row, the Americans reached the gold-medal game. Just as it did in 2000, the final was decided in extra time. The United States and Brazil had played to a 1–1 tie. But the younger Brazilians were still going strong. Hamm and the Americans were struggling to keep up. Then, in the 112th minute, the US team got a corner kick. Most of the attention in Athens had been on the US veterans. But it was the team's brightest young star who played the hero. Abby Wambach jumped into the air and smashed a header

ICONIC BRAZILIANS

In 2024, Brazil's women's team reached its third Olympic gold-medal game. Although the team lost in all three finals, its players provided plenty of thrills. In 2021, Marta became the first player to score in five consecutive Olympics. Nobody has scored more Olympic goals than Cristiane's 14. That included three goals in 14 minutes against Nigeria in 2008. And 43-year-old midfielder Formiga played in her seventh Games in 2021. That made her the first soccer player to take part in seven Olympics.

into the net. Thanks to that goal, the Fab Five went out as gold medalists.

The US dynasty continued after Athens. But nothing came easy. Women's soccer was becoming more and more competitive. In Brazil, the dazzling playmaker Marta had emerged as the world's best player. Meanwhile, Germany won back-to-back Women's World Cups in 2003 and 2007. So it didn't look good for the US team when Wambach broke her leg prior to the 2008 Games in Beijing, China. Without their star, the Americans lost their Olympic opener.

The loss could have spelled disaster for the Americans. But as the tournament went on, the team found ways to grind out wins. And once again, the Americans reached the final. Facing Brazil, US goalie Hope Solo played lights out. First-time Olympian Carli Lloyd scored in extra time to give the Americans a 1–0 victory.

Four years later, the United States and Canada met in the 2012 Olympic semifinals. The contest was called an instant classic. Canada's star forward Christine Sinclair scored three goals during the game. But each time, the US team answered back. Dynamic winger Megan Rapinoe scored twice. The first came on a corner kick. Her looping kick confused the defenders and skipped right into the goal. Wambach tied it on a penalty kick in the 80th minute.

Megan Rapinoe, *left*, finished the 2012 Games with three goals and four assists to help Team USA win its fourth gold medal.

With each passing minute, the teams seemed to take the action to a higher and higher level. It finally ended in extra time. With seconds to play before a shootout, young American forward Alex Morgan got her head on a cross. The ball flew just beyond the goalie's reach and into the net. The US team had once again survived Olympic play.

That win set up an anticipated final against Japan. It was a rematch of the previous year's Women's World Cup final, which Japan won. More than 80,000 fans filled Wembley Stadium for the gold-medal match. Once again, Lloyd stepped up on the big stage, scoring twice. Japan got one back, but it was not enough. The United States won 2–1 to claim a third consecutive gold medal.

NEW ERA, NEW STARS

Sweden finally put an end to the US dynasty at the 2016 Olympics. The longtime rivals met in the quarterfinals. After a 1–1 draw, Sweden moved on with a 4–3 win in a shootout.

The United States had never fallen short of the semifinals at a major tournament. Without the Americans, the tournament was wide open. None of the final four teams had won Olympic gold before. In the end, Germany held off Sweden 2–1 in the final in Rio.

The next Olympic tournament brought more surprises. At the Tokyo, Japan, Olympics in 2021, Sweden stunned the top-ranked US team with a 3–0 win in the opener. The Americans needed a shootout to get past the Netherlands in the quarterfinals. But in the semifinals, Canada finally got its revenge from the 2012 Olympics.

Through the first 73 minutes, neither team could break through. Then Canada's Jessie Fleming slammed a penalty kick into the corner of the net. The goal held up as Canada beat the United States 1–0. Afterward, the Canadians laughed and cheered at midfield. The US players, on the other hand, could only look on in shock.

A few days later, Canada met Sweden in the women's Olympic final. This time, Fleming scored to tie the game 1–1. Canada then secured the gold medal in a shootout. After back-to-back bronze medals, Canada joined the club of Olympic champions.

Members of Canada's women's soccer team rush to celebrate after defeating Sweden in a penalty shootout at the Tokyo Games in 2021.

CAPTAIN CHRISTINE

Even at 38 years old, Christine Sinclair remained Canada's captain and biggest star at the Tokyo Games in 2021. Through the 2024 Games, no player in international soccer history has scored more goals than Sinclair. Although she had no goals in the Olympic final against Sweden in 2021, she did draw a second-half penalty.

BACK ON TOP

Nearly 44,000 fans packed into the Parc des Princes in Paris on August 10, 2024. The US team, seeking its first Olympic gold medal in 12 years, needed to get past an old rival. Brazil had fallen off since winning the 2008 Olympic silver medal. But suddenly, the Brazilians were on a roll. So were the Americans. The 2024 final quickly became a thrilling clash.

Each team traded scoring chances in the first half. Twelve minutes into the second, Mallory Swanson broke toward the goal. Swanson had long been seen as one of the United States' next great goal-scorers. A serious knee injury in 2023 threatened to derail her career. But she was back in time for the 2024 Games. Alongside fellow forwards Trinity Rodman and Sophia Smith, Swanson had helped lead Team USA back to the gold-medal match.

In the 57th minute, Team USA's Korbin Albert sent a long pass toward Brazil's penalty area. Swanson reached the ball, tapped it twice, and then slid a perfect shot under Brazil's goalkeeper to put the United States ahead by one. In stoppage

Team USA's Mallory Swanson, *right*, scores the lone goal in the 2024 Olympic women's soccer final.

time, US goalie Alyssa Naeher made a diving, one-handed stop to keep Brazil off the board. Finally, the whistle blew. With a hard-fought 1–0 win, the US women were on top of the podium for a record fifth time.

GLOSSARY

amateur
A person who plays a sport without getting paid.

club
The team a player competes with outside of his or her national team.

debut
First appearance.

dynasty
A team that has an extended period of success, usually winning multiple championships in the process.

extra time
Two 15-minute periods added to a tournament game if the score is tied at the end of regulation.

group stage
The part of a tournament when teams are divided into smaller groups or pools; each team faces the others in its group, and those with the best records move on to the knockout stage.

own goal
A goal that is accidentally scored by a player against his or her own team.

professional
A person who gets paid to perform.

rival
An opponent with whom a player or team has a fierce and ongoing competition.

segregated
When groups of people are separated based on race, gender, ethnicity, or other factors.

shootout
A series of penalty kicks held after extra time to decide who wins a game.

stoppage time
Also known as injury time, a number of minutes tacked on to the end of a half for stoppages that occurred during play because of injuries, free kicks, and goals.

underdog
The person or team that is not expected to win.

veterans
Athletes who have played for many years.

MORE INFORMATION

BOOKS

Clarke, David J. *Everything Soccer.* Abdo, 2024.

Hewson, Anthony K. *GOATs of Soccer.* Abdo, 2022.

Stevenson, Robin. *Kid Olympians, Summer.* Quirk Books, 2024.

ONLINE RESOURCES

Booklinks
NONFICTION NETWORK
FREE! ONLINE NONFICTION RESOURCES

To learn more about Olympic soccer, please visit **abdobooklinks.com** or scan this QR code. These links are routinely monitored and updated to provide the most current information available.

INDEX

ABOUT THE AUTHOR

Chrös McDougall is a sportswriter, author, and book editor who focuses on Olympic and Paralympic sports. A lifelong soccer fan, he has written about the sport for various publications and covered the US women's team at the 2021 Olympic Games in Tokyo, Japan. He also witnessed Lionel Messi and Argentina win the Olympic gold medal in 2008. McDougall lives in Minneapolis, Minnesota, with his wife, two children, and a soccer playing boxer named Eira.